BUILDING
WEALTH IN THE
STOCK MARKET

The Basics of Investing

DISCLAIMER

This book is for educational purposes only and is not affiliated with any financial institution. The information provided is not investment advice and does not provide recommendations to potential investors. This book's contents shall not be construed as financial, tax, legal advice, or other, and might be outdated or inaccurate as time passes. The names of actual companies mentioned may be trademarks of their respective owners. Do your own due diligence when making any type of investment. Please consult your financial adviser before beginning to invest or make monetary decisions. All rights reserved. No part of this book may be reproduced or used in any form or by any means without the author's prior written permission.

TABLE OF CONTENTS

INTRODUCTION

There are many ways to build wealth over time, and one of the most accessible ways is through the stock market. However, the stock market can be intimidating when you have little to no knowledge of how it works. While investing in stocks is an excellent way to make money, it is not an overnight get-rich-quick scheme; it takes patience and understanding. This book will teach you the fundamentals to get started investing in the stock market to grow your wealth and net worth over time. You will learn the basics of the stock market, the benefits of investing in stocks, some key investing terms, the different ways to invest, the different types of investments, investing strategies, how to value a stock, and how to think like an intelligent investor. Billionaire investor and entrepreneur Warren Buffet preaches that the best investment you can make is an investment in yourself. Teaching yourself new skills and reading books like this will increase your chances of becoming financially successful in your future.

BENEFITS OF INVESTING

It is common to hear that many people make money from investing, but there are many more benefits than just that. Most people will work until they retire and then live off of social security, but as you may know, that usually is not enough. Investing over the years has the potential to set you up so that you can have more money saved when you retire and live very comfortably. If you start consistently investing early enough in your life, you may even be able to retire early. For many people, achieving financial freedom is a lifetime goal. Financial freedom is defined as having enough money coming in from your investments and assets so that you no longer need to work at a job because all of your expenses are covered. Sticking to this path and continuing to invest in assets that generate income is a large part of why the rich keep getting richer. Setting up a stock investment portfolio is one of the main ways people reach financial freedom. It is essential to understand that any kind of investing has varying levels of risk. You are never guaranteed to make money; in some cases, you may lose money. This is why it is important to understand how to invest and what to invest your money in. This book will cover what to look for when you pick out individual stocks to buy so you can have an idea of what makes for a good investment.

A critical factor in investing that many people forget to consider is that not investing, or waiting too long to invest, can cost you a lot of money. This is because of two main factors; the first one is inflation. Inflation simply means that the number of goods your money can buy is less, and therefore your money has less purchasing power. You often hear that the price of a gallon of milk twenty years ago was less than what it costs today, and this is why a $10 bill can buy you less today than it could back then. According to an article from thebalance.com, the average inflation rate from 2010 to 2019 is 1.76% (Amadeo, 2020). While this is a relatively small amount, it can quickly add up over time. If you take this average inflation rate over forty years, your money will lose about half its value When it becomes time to retire, the amount of money you thought you would need may not be enough. This is why a savings account should just be used to store enough money to cover your living expenses in case of an emergency or loss of income. However, everything past that should be invested to prevent your buying power from being destroyed by inflation.

The second factor that illustrates how waiting to invest could be costing you money is known as opportunity cost. This is closely linked to the concept of compounding, which will be explained later, and the time value of money. The time value of money can be explained as the fact that money today is more valuable than money in the future. For example, if you could choose between receiving $1,000 today or $1,000 in one year, the first option is more beneficial. If you take the money right away and invest, assuming that you got a 5% return and did not put any more money into your stock portfolio, after one year, that $1,000 would have grown to $1,050. You used your money to generate more money and made $50. While this may not sound like a lot, this is where compounding comes into play. That first year you made a return of $50, but in the second year, you will make $52.50, the third year will be 55.13, and so on. This is known as compounding because the money starts to grow exponentially, creating a snowball effect. This is why it is highly beneficial to start investing early, because the more time you have, the faster your money grows. As another example, if you start putting away $500 per month into a savings account at age twenty-five, in thirty years, you will have saved $180,000. However, if you invested that same $500 for the same amount of time, assuming a modest 5% average annual return, you will have a balance of $409,308.92. Your contribution was still $180,000, but now you also accumulated an additional $229,348.92 in gains.

If you had the option to receive a million dollars or double a penny for thirty straight days, which would you choose? Many people would take the million dollars without a second thought. However, if you do the math, a penny doubled for thirty days straight comes out to be over five million dollars or $5,368,709.12 to be exact, and the chart below illustrates this. While the chances of finding an investment that will continually double in value daily are slim to none, this example serves to illustrate the power of compounding money over time. This is why Albert Einstein referred to compounding as the eighth wonder of the world (Bendel, 2017).

Day 1	0.1		Day 16	327.68
Day 2	0.2		Day 17	655.36
Day 3	0.4		Day 18	1,310.72
Day 4	0.8		Day 19	2,621.44
Day 5	0.16		Day 20	5,242.88
Day 6	0.32		Day 21	10,485.76
Day 7	0.64		Day 22	20,971.52
Day 8	1.28		Day 23	41,943.04
Day 9	2.56		Day 24	83,866.08
Day 10	5.12		Day 25	167,772.16
Day 11	10.24		Day 26	335,544.32
Day 12	20.48		Day 27	671,088.64
Day 13	40.96		Day 28	1,342,177.28
Day 14	81.94		Day 29	2,684,354.56
Day 15	163.84		Day 30	5,368,709.12

THE STOCK MARKET & KEY TERMS

The stock market is a marketplace that allows you to buy shares, which are fractions of a business, that are available for the average person to own, essentially making you one of the owners of the company. You can buy shares of companies like McDonald's, Apple, and Facebook, and the general idea is that when these companies do well their overall value increases. This will cause the stock price, or the price of each share, to increase and make money for the people who own shares when they decide to sell those shares. You can also make money with dividends, but this will be explained further in later chapters. When getting into the world of investing, there will be some recurring terms you will see. The most common terms are defined below:

- IPO - This stands for Initial Public Offering, which is when a business's shares become available to the general public to invest in the business. This is when people can collectively buy and sell shares to make money.

- Portfolio - Your portfolio is simply your collection of investments. A stock portfolio can consist of as many or as few stocks as you want.

- Diversification - This is the practice of spreading your investments across multiple companies or industries to minimize risk so that you are not as affected by one stock or asset's performance.

- Bull Market - This is when the economy is doing well, the stock market as a whole is doing well, and stock prices are generally going up. You can also be bullish on an individual stock if you believe the company will do well in the coming years.

- Bear Market - This is when the stock market is in a downturn, and stock prices are going down consistently. A bear market is typically marked by a 20% decline from recent levels. Things that can accompany a bear market are high unemployment rates, and many people panic selling all of their investments, which only add to share prices dropping.

- Ticker symbol - The ticker symbol, also known as the stock symbol, is an abbreviation for the stock, usually between one and four letters. This is just a shorthand way of referencing a company's stock. For example, the ticker symbol for Amazon is AMZN. Typing this symbol into a brokerage account will bring up the company's details and financials, as well as where you can buy or sell the stock.

- Equity - Regarding stocks, equity is defined as the amount of money left over when you subtract the company's liabilities from its assets; this is the actual cash value of the business if it were to close its doors and liquidate everything.

- Blue-chip stock - Blue-chip stocks refer to massive companies that have been around for decades. They are usually worth at least a billion dollars and are typically industry leaders. These are well-established businesses that are historically secure, have a solid reputation for excellent management, and offer consistent dividend payments to their investors. Some examples are Disney, IBM, and Coca-Cola.

- Penny stocks - Penny stocks are smaller companies that usually trade for less than $5 per share. There is higher upside potential, and a higher level of risk involved because these are smaller businesses that have not been proven yet, and it is not certain that they will succeed or even stay in business. Penny stocks are also known as OTC or over-the-counter stocks.

- Stock split - This is when a company will either increase or decrease the number of outstanding shares (the total number of shares available to the public) to increase or decrease its stock price. A forward split is when companies increase the number of shares, and therefore the share price is lower. Fundamentally, there is no change in value. If you hold one share of company A valued at $100, and it does a four to one forward split, you will gain three additional shares for a total of four, and each share will be valued at $25. You will still have the same amount of money invested but with more shares. The benefit of a stock split is that more people will be able to buy into a company if they have less money to invest at one time. A company that does very well may have a share price in the thousands, but after a split, it is now just a few hundred, and that could be a more manageable amount for the average person to start investing with that business.

- Reverse stock split - A reverse stock split is the opposite of a stock split. This is when a company consolidates the outstanding shares so that there are fewer of them, each worth more money. This is usually done because if a company's share price falls below $1 for too long, it could be delisted on stock exchanges and would no longer be publicly traded. This is why there is generally a negative connotation around reverse stock splits.

GETTING STARTED
WITH INVESTING

In this day and age, it is the easiest it has ever been to get involved in stock market investing. There used to be this idea that you could only invest if you were rich, but that is simply not true today. Anyone with a smartphone can download an app and start investing with a minimal amount of money. To start trading in the stock market, you need to open a brokerage account, which is like a bank account that is used to buy and sell shares of companies. There are several reputable companies you can use, and as mentioned before, most of them have very user-friendly apps that can quickly and easily be downloaded on your phone. Some examples are Vanguard, Robinhood, Webull, and M1 Finance. These are all viable options as most of them offer zero commission trading. It used to be the industry-standard practice to pay a stockbroker a commission whenever you wanted to buy or sell shares within a brokerage account. As you can imagine, these fees would quickly eat into any profits you received. Regardless of which option you choose, you must look at what fees they charge and preferably go with one that has no commission fees for trades. A lot of these brokerage accounts have a referral bonus as well, so if you have a friend who already has an account, you can get their referral code, and both of you can get a free stock or some other incentive.

When starting to invest, there are a few things to consider. While there are ways to decrease your risk, some level of risk is involved with every kind of investing. This is why it is important to invest only what you can afford to live without. Investing your life savings into a new company can be a recipe for disaster. Invest only what you can afford and ensure you still have enough cash and liquid assets in the event of an emergency. If you lose that entire investment, it should not negatively affect your everyday lifestyle.

TYPES OF INVESTMENTS

There are different types of assets into which you can invest. These include stocks, mutual funds, index funds, ETFs (Exchange Traded Funds), bonds, and REITs (Real Estate Investment Trusts). There are also different investment strategies such as active investing, passive investing, and inactive investing. Each of these options will be explored, as well as how they work.

First, there are stocks. Once you have a brokerage account, you can pick individual stocks to buy and sell, and this is known as active investing. As mentioned earlier, when you buy shares of a business, you can get paid based on two factors: when the value of the stock you own increases, and when you get dividends for owning the stock. First, there is what is known as stock appreciation. Here is an example: if you bought five shares of a company and each share cost $20 when you bought it, this means that your initial investment into this business was $100. Assume that nine months go by and that company grows, and each share is now worth $40. This means that it doubled in value, and your initial investment of $100 is now worth $200, so you were able to double your money because you made a good investment. If you were to sell your shares at that particular moment, you would receive $200 because that is the current value for that stock.

Another way that people make money from the stock market is through dividends. This is when businesses pay their investors a quarterly payment (sometimes it may be monthly) for the shares they own. This amount is a percentage based on how many shares you own in that company. This is essentially free money that you make just for holding the stock. You can also set up what is known as a Dividend Reinvestment Plan, also known as DRIP. This method sets up the payments you get in the form of dividends to be automatically reinvested, causing your money to compound and grow even faster as time passes.

While looking at stocks, it can be tricky to figure out where to invest your money. For those who may not have the time or patience to do the research necessary to pick good companies, diversified options become very attractive. These consist of mutual funds, index funds, and ETFs, and they are either actively or passively managed. These are easier options for beginners looking to start with investing.

First, there are mutual funds, and these are made up of a collection of companies in which you can invest just by buying that one fund. The benefit of a mutual fund is the instant diversification since the average fund has about ninety stocks within it. Therefore, you are not putting all of your eggs in one basket, and you will lower your risk when investing. Mutual funds are also actively managed, which means that they are managed by a professional known as a fund manager or a team of fund managers. They adjust the stocks kept within the fund regularly as needed, and their primary goal is to outperform the overall stock market growth and make money for their investors. However, it is important to note the negative aspects of mutual funds.

As mentioned previously, a mutual fund is actively managed, and the people responsible for managing the fund get paid via the fees that you must pay. The fees vary based on the mutual fund, but they can go up to 2% per year. While this may not sound like a lot, these fees can result in the investor losing tens of thousands of dollars over the years and decades. Furthermore, these fees still apply regardless of the fund's performance, meaning that even if you, the investor, lose money one year, you still pay that fee. The cost associated with managing the fund is known as the expense ratio. Typically, you will get a lower expense ratio from passively managed funds than actively managed funds.

This transitions into index funds, which are a type of mutual fund, but with a few key differences. The stocks and assets within this type of fund are picked based on a market indicator, otherwise known as an index. An index is a collection of stocks that is typically used as a baseline for determining how the overall stock market is doing or how a certain sector is doing. You cannot invest directly into an index, so you invest in these collections by buying into index funds. Index funds are passively managed because they track an index rather than being managed by a person or team. A good example of this and probably the most popular index to track is the S&P 500 (Standard & Poor's). This index tracks the top five hundred companies in the United States and is updated regularly. The S&P 500 goes hand in hand with two other major indexes in the US: the Nasdaq and the Dow Jones Industrials (DJI). The Nasdaq is composed of over three thousand stocks, with a very high concentration of technology stocks, so shifts in the tech industry will weigh heavily in this index. The Dow Jones index is only made up of about thirty stocks, but they are among the largest companies traded in America. These are the blue-chip stocks outlined earlier and include large companies from almost every sector, excluding utilities and transportation. Many analysts will often look at these three major indexes to assess the health of the overall stock market.

The S&P 500, however, is typically seen as the best single indicator of the U.S. economy. Within the S&P 500 index, you will often hear about the acronym FAANG, and this is composed of some of the largest companies within the index: Facebook, Apple, Amazon, Netflix, and Google. Occasionally you will see this acronym as FAANGM, which is when Microsoft is included. These companies are so large that their performance can affect the performance of the entire index. To reiterate, index funds are passively managed, and as you know, passively managed funds have a lower expense ratio. The average expense ratio is typically around 0.2%, and, in some cases, it is even as low as 0.02%. One important aspect of both mutual funds and index funds is that both of these funds often have a minimum amount required to invest within them, and this can be anywhere from a few hundred dollars to a few thousand and beyond. This way, you can invest in a fund that fits your budget and how much you have to invest.

A top-rated index fund is Vanguard's S&P 500 index, and its ticker symbol is VFIAX. At the time of writing, this fund has a minimum required investment of $3,000 and an expense ratio of 0.04%. As an example of how this expense ratio works, for every $10,000 you have invested in this fund, you will pay a fee of $4 per year. Investing in this fund gives you exposure to the S&P 500 index and a simple way to invest in some of the US's best companies in one place. In many cases, the S&P 500 outperforms some of the most advanced active fund managers over the long term. Over a period of ten years, the S&P 500 performed better than 85% of actively managed funds (Pisani, 2019).

Next, there are ETFs, which are exchange-traded funds. These are versatile funds, and they function as a normal stock that can be traded during normal market hours. A major benefit of ETFs is that they have no minimum required to invest, and they can often be as cheap as roughly $38 to buy one "share" of them. An example of an ETF like this is the PowerShares S&P 500 High Dividend Low Volatility ETF, and its ticker symbol is SPHD. This particular ETF tracks fifty of the least volatile businesses within the S&P 500's seventy-five highest dividend-paying companies. This allows more people to start investing because if they only have $100 to invest, instead of having to go with an index fund that has a minimum of $3,000, they now have the option to buy $100 worth of ETFs that track the same companies and start investing at their own pace.

ETFs also typically have low expense ratios that are comparable to index funds; however, it is still important to check the expense ratio before you invest. Many ETFs mirror popular index funds, such as those that track the S&P 500, and even have a similar inexpensive expense ratio. For example, if you want to be exposed to the S&P 500 index but do not have the minimum deposit for the index fund, there is another popular vanguard ETF, ticker symbol VOO, that tracks the same stocks as the index fund VFIAX. This ETF has no minimum requirements and has an expense ratio of 0.03%. Therefore, ETFs can be a way to invest and diversify your stock portfolio with relative ease and start building towards your long-term goals. For beginners, mutual funds, index funds, and ETFs are arguably the easiest ways to get started with investing.

Inactive investing is when you invest on an automated set schedule. The most common example of this is if you opt into a 401K through your employer, and they take money out of each paycheck, so you do not see that money. Some employers will often match up to a certain percentage of your contributions, which is essentially free money. Something to note, though, this type of investing can have higher expense ratios that can cost as much as a third of your profits over the years. So as always, ensure this is something you look into before you invest this way.

Next, there are bonds. A bond is when you loan money to an entity such as a business; however, the most common forms of bonds are government bonds. You get paid back with interest from the entity you loaned the money to. Bonds are generally safer investments in most cases, and it is good to have a percentage of your portfolio in bonds. The level of risk associated with a bond depends on the entity; a startup company trying to raise capital is a lot more of a risky investment than a well-established business that has been around and successful for decades. A riskier company will compensate for this by offering a higher interest rate on its bond, making the potential payoff more lucrative. As mentioned earlier, the time value of money is critical. While it can be a good idea to have a smaller percentage of your portfolio in bonds for diversity, it is common for people to shift more of their money into safer investments as they get closer to retirement to avoid short-term volatility right before they will need to withdraw their money. Investments with some calculated risk involved can be excellent in building wealth, but safer investments are great for maintaining wealth.

Lastly, there are REITs, real estate investment trusts. This is a way to invest in real estate without having to worry about maintaining a property, managing tenants, or having a large initial investment to pay for the down payment. One major benefit of REITs is that they typically have a high dividend yield because they are required by law to pay their investors at least 90% of their profits. REITs can be bought and sold on the stock market within a brokerage account, making them easily accessible. Just like with stocks, if you do not want to invest in one singular company, you can invest in REIT ETFs, which are diversified options that invest in many different REITs so you can have a balanced portfolio. One of the downsides of REITs is that the income you receive from these dividends is taxed as ordinary income, the same as the tax you pay from your employment income. This is not ideal because you can get taxed less depending on how you invest. In the next chapter, you will learn the different ways investments are taxed.

INVESTING STRATEGIES

There are many different strategies you can use to invest in the stock market. The first method, and arguably the easiest way to be successful, is to consistently invest over the long term, also known as the buy and hold method. This is when you buy shares of fundamentally sound companies and hold onto them for many years, if not decades. There are many reasons why this method is held in high regard, but three will be focused on here. One of the reasons this method is highly effective is illustrated in the example given in the opening chapter when discussing compounding. You are allowing your contributions to grow significantly faster with the time that passes. The money will also grow more quickly if the business you invest in pays out a dividend that you automatically invest back into the business's stock, providing more money with which the balance can grow exponentially.

The second benefit to long term investing is that you do not have to worry about short term fluctuations within the stock market. The overall markets are up and down, and every so often, you will experience things like recessions, market crashes, and economic hardships. It is crucial to understand that these things are not only inevitable, but they are also normal. If you are following the long-term investing method, these fluctuations are largely irrelevant. Economic downturns like these can be an amazing opportunity for experienced investors to make money. As mentioned earlier, the S&P 500 is not only an indicator of the performance of the overall stock market, but it is one of the most popular indexes to invest in. According to a CNBC article, this index's average annual return over the past ninety years is just under 10% (Santoli, 2017). With this knowledge in mind, when a year passes and your return is minimal or even negative, understand that in the long term, it is likely to average out in your favor. This is where the old ideology that many millionaires are created in times of economic hardships comes from.

The last benefit to investing over the long term that will be explored is the tax benefit. As with any type of income, you must pay a percentage of it in taxes. Stock market gains are taxed in one of two ways, and these are short-term capital gains tax and long-term capital gains tax. If you sell a stock within one year of buying it, you pay a short-term capital gains tax. This tax is the same as the percentage of your normal tax rate on your income. "The long-term rates are 0 percent, 15 percent, or 20 percent, depending on your tax bracket. Individuals who make less than $39,375 and married couples who earn less than $78,750 pay no taxes on long-term capital gains. Individuals who earn $39,376 to $434,550 (and married couples earning $78,751 to $488,850) pay 15 percent in long-term capital gains taxes. And taxpayers earning more than that are required to pay 20 percent of their long-term capital gains in taxes." (Jackson, 2019).

In most cases, the short-term capital gains tax is higher than the long-term capital gains tax, further incentivizing you to hold onto shares for a longer period. While on the subject of taxes, this is a good time to discuss realized and unrealized gains. If you hold onto a stock, and it doubles in value, but you are still holding it and have not sold any of those shares, this is called an unrealized gain. You do not have to pay taxes on unrealized gains, only on realized gains, which is when you sell shares at a profit.

Some other ways to invest in stocks include day trading and options trading. It is *extremely* important to note that these methods typically carry significantly more risk, and it is recommended that you have a profound understanding of how they work before you start to invest your hard-earned money into them. Due to this, these trading methods will only be briefly discussed here. Day trading is when you buy and sell stocks frequently within a short amount of time to make a quick profit. This process often happens multiple times within a day, as the name implies. This is arguably a full-time job in itself, as you must monitor many different metrics and market indicators and be ready to execute a trade at any given moment. As for options trading, this is when you buy a contract that gives you the right to buy or sell shares of a company at a later time. You are essentially making a bet that the stock price will go up or down in the future, and if you are correct, you can close out your position, also known as exercising your contract, for a profit. Of course, this is an extremely oversimplified explanation of options trading, but again, these are examples of investing strategies that will not be investigated too deeply here.

HOW TO VALUE STOCKS

When it comes time to pick stocks within your portfolio, you want to ensure that you pick companies that are the most likely to make you money and increase your net worth, but to do this, you must understand how to value them. If you chose to invest in an index fund or ETF, it is relatively straight-forward. Since these are already diversified funds, your decision will be based on what sector you want to invest in, what index you want to have exposure to, and factors like the expense ratio. Many investors will invest pas-sively through something like an index fund or an ETF, as it takes a lot of the hassle out of investing while still yielding a solid return. However, when picking individ-ual stocks, there are a few more things to consider, and this takes a lot more patience.

It is important to understand that while the following covers how to value a business and its stock fundamen-tally, the overall stock market is very reactionary. There is a lot of emotion involved. A wise investor does not act on emotion. Intrinsic value is a term used to describe the fair price for a company's stock, and this can give you an excellent idea as to what you should reasonably pay for each share. There are many methods used to calculate the intrinsic value of a stock, such as the asset-based valuation, analysis based on a financial metric, or the discounted cash flow analysis, to name a few. Asset-based valuation is relatively simple; you subtract the business's total liabilities from its total assets. Values that can be found on the financial statements will be explored in this chapter. Analysis based on a financial metric is when a metric is used, such as the P/E (Price/Earnings) ratio, to calculate the intrinsic value. When using the P/E ratio, the equation would be: (EPS) x (1 + r) x P/E ratio = intrinsic value. R's value in this equation would be the expected earnings growth rate, and the EPS is earnings per share. Both the P/E ratio and EPS will be discussed in further detail later in this chapter. Finally, there is a process known as the discounted cash flow (DCF) analysis, which is one of the more complex methods. This method involves three steps:

1. Estimate all of a company's future cash flows.
2. Calculate the present value of each of these future cash flows.
3. Sum up the present values to obtain the intrinsic value of the stock.

You will need to get estimates for future cash flows based on values taken from financial statements like the cash flow statement, which will be covered later in this chapter. Cash flows may change in the future, so it is important to understand the business's potential for growth to make educated guesses. Once you have these values, the formula to calculate the intrinsic value using the DCF analysis is as follows: $(CF_n)/(1 + r)^n$ (Speights, 2020).

Expanded, the equation would look like this: $(CF1)/(1 + r)^1 + (CF2)/(1 + r)^2 + (CF3)/(1 + r)^3$ etc. CF1 would represent cash flow in year one, and CF2 would be cash flow in year two, and so on. R would be the hypothetical rate of return you could get elsewhere, and N represents the year. Regardless of the method used to determine the intrinsic value, it is important to understand that this value is an estimate rather than a concrete number. While the various methods of determining the intrinsic value can be confusing, the core concept can be boiled down to this: the value of a stock should be based on the fundamentals and financials of the actual business, instead of the current price of the stock (Speights, 2020).

The principle of intrinsic value is a staple in value investing. Some of the most successful investors like Warren Buffet are value investors, which means that they look to buy shares in strong, high performing companies that are trading at a price below their intrinsic value. They make their money when the stock price rises back up to its expected level, the intrinsic value. Due to the somewhat emotional nature of the stock market mentioned earlier, there are many times when the price of a stock does not reflect what is happening within the company.

A business may be doing very well, is profitable, and comfortably growing market share, but the stock price has dropped 20% within the last six months. This may have been for several reasons, many of which are out of the company's control, such as a global pandemic, an election that generally causes high volatility in the markets, or political tension between different countries. However, this presents an amazing opportunity for value investors. They will take this time to buy valuable companies at a discount, so to speak, and can potentially get a return of at least around 20% on their money in this example. The idea is that the actual business model and results should be analyzed, not the stock price. If the numbers and fundamentals are solid, the stock price will correct back to its intrinsic value in time. Therefore, the short-term volatility will be irrelevant. Value investors typically invest their money over the long term to maximize their gains. Stocks usually fall under one of two categories, value stocks and growth stocks. The next section will look at different ways to evaluate value stocks.

How do you figure out what a business is worth as a whole? There are many different metrics that can be used to value a stock, also known as multiples. Many kinds of multiples exist, and some are even specific to a certain industry, but the focus in this text will be on the most relevant ones that are the most widely used. The first focus will be on market capitalization. This is determined by taking the current price of that company's shares and multiplying that number by the number of outstanding shares available. In most cases, you will not need to calculate the market capitalization as it will be provided by the brokerage account you use or through a quick online search. Market capitalization is also referred to as market valuation. In an ideal world, a company's valuation is based on its fundamentals, such as its assets, revenues, and overall business model. However, it is not uncommon for a company to be overvalued due to excitement around its future potential or undervalued if the average investors and analysts do not fully understand the business or the competitive advantages it has in the market.

The next multiple used to help determine the intrinsic value of a stock is known as the P/E ratio, which was discussed earlier. This stands for the Price to Earnings ratio. The P/E ratio is a way to value a stock based on the amount of revenue the business makes. You are comparing the share price to its earnings, which is the money it brings in minus the business expenses, and using this metric to determine the value of the stock you are buying. The two variations of this that will be explored are the trailing P/E ratio and the forward P/E ratio. People often look to the past as an indicator of how a business may perform, which is why it is called a trailing P/E ratio. This is determined by taking the current price per share of a company and dividing it by the sum of that company's EPS (earnings per share) for the past four quarters, or twelve months. Here is an example: if you take company A and see that it has a current share price of $20 per share and that the last four quarters' EPS was $1.25, the trailing P/E ratio is 16. This means that the price of company A's stock is 16 times its earnings.

Next, there is the forward P/E ratio, and this is when you look at what the business will be valued at based on the projected future growth. The difference here is that you are dividing the share price by the estimated EPS for the upcoming four quarters. Suppose company A is projected to grow its revenue over the next twelve months for an estimated EPS of $3.25, assuming the same share price of $20. In that case, you will divide that by $3.25 to get a forward P/E ratio of approximately 6.15. The forward P/E is more speculative as the EPS can vary when compared to expectations. Hence, it is imperative to understand this is only an estimate of future potential for the business. The trailing P/E ratio is more accurate;

however, a stock's past performance does not inherently mean the future performance will be the same. The forward P/E ratio, while speculative, can provide you with a benchmark on what to expect for the short-term future of the company's financials. The trailing P/E ratio is usually made available to you on the details page in the brokerage account you are using, so you will normally not have to do these equations yourself. The EPS can be taken directly from the business's income statement, which will be discussed in further detail later in this chapter.

Another important point is that the P/E ratio is best used as a benchmark when comparing companies within the same industry. Many people generally believe that the lower the P/E ratio of a business, the better, with a P/E ratio under twenty-five to be best, but this is not always the case, and the stock market is not that simple. Companies in the tech industry, for example, are known to have much higher P/E ratios. This is because fast-growing companies often have future growth factored into their share price, with the expectation that the company's revenue will rise to meet these numbers. A promising upcoming company in this sector could have a significantly higher P/E ratio because there is a lot of excitement around the stock and many people buying into it because they see it growing rapidly in the upcoming months and years. On paper, this can make the business look overvalued, but if it grows on pace with expectations, there can still be plenty of room to grow.

If a business does not have a P/E ratio listed, this means that it is not profitable yet. This is not too uncommon because businesses often have hefty upfront costs to get up and running and may not see a profit for several years. In addition, companies that are focused on rapid growth often will not post profits because any profits made are just funneled back into the business to focus on expanding as quickly as possible. This can be building new store locations or factories or increasing production to meet the demand for their products. Taking this approach can allow a relatively young business to go from not being profitable to being one of the bigger players in that industry in a short time, once it transitions from a growth phase and starts posting profits consistently.

The next multiple is the price to sales ratio. This is used to compare the share price to the company sales. The price to sales ratio can be determined by dividing the total market capitalization by the total revenue. While the P/E ratio deals with earnings, which is profits after the business expenses are deducted, the price to sales ratio deals with the total revenue, or sales, before deductions. Earnings can be easier to manipulate than sales, making the price to sales ratio more popular among some investors. This can be useful to determine if a business is growing its customer base and market share annually and help with future predictions. This multiple has drawbacks as well, just like any other one. Sales do not equal profits, so it is still important to look at earnings as well. When looking at this multiple, the general idea is that a price to sales ratio below one is ideal, but as mentioned before, these values can vary based on the industry you are looking at.

Finally, there is the P/B ratio or price to book ratio. This is also known as the price to equity ratio. This is a method of valuing a business based on its total assets. If you take the difference of the total assets and liabilities and divide this number by the number of outstanding shares, the answer you are left with is the book value per share or BVPS. Using the book value per share, you can now calculate the price to book ratio. The formula for this is the share price divided by the BVPS. The idea with this multiple is that a business with a very high P/B ratio is overvalued, and one with a low P/B ratio is undervalued. A value investor will typically look for a P/B ratio under three. However, much like with the P/E ratio, a good P/B ratio will vary based on the industry you are looking at. It is a good idea to research the average for the industry that you are considering investing in.

There are pros and cons to using any multiple to value a stock, and this is why it is good to avoid settling for just one. Imagine a business manufactures a product but

then struggles to meet the demand for said product because it cannot make the products quickly enough. The
company decides to buy a new machine for each of its
factories that can manufacture significantly more of the
product in a much faster time. This machine is a great
asset for the business, making it more profitable in the
future, but it is a very costly business investment in the
short term. When they report their earnings, they will
likely be lower due to the expense of adding these new
machines; however, their sales will have gone up exponentially because they are finally able to make enough
products to keep up with demand. In this scenario, if
you look solely at the trailing P/E ratio, you may see
subpar earnings and think this company may not be a
good investment. However, if you look at the price to
sales ratio, you can see that their revenue is quickly increasing since they can finally catch up with demand.

Another pro when looking at the price to sales ratio
is when analyzing cyclical businesses, which are companies that do well in a certain season or time frame.
For example, if a company typically has little to no
earnings during the winter months, it is normal for revenues to rise and fall, which will affect the P/E ratio.
However, if you look at the price to sales ratio, you can
see that sales are increasing year over year, and this can
give you a better understanding of how the company
is doing overall. With that said, the price to sales ratio
can be tricky if that is your main focus. If a business

is poorly managed, it might be generating revenue, but it is not profitable and is using debt to conduct business operations. As mentioned earlier, sometimes a business may not post a profit because it is reinvesting the money into its growth, but this is very different from a business that cannot turn a profit at all. To reiterate, these are some of the reasons why it is best to look at more than one multiple when valuing a stock. These multiples are best viewed as pieces of a puzzle; the more you look, the clearer the overall picture will be.

There are many financial statements that you can analyze to understand the financial health of a business, but the focus here will be on three main ones: the income statement, the cash flow statement, and the balance sheet. The first that will be analyzed is the income statement. This statement illustrates a company's net income during a certain period, such as quarterly or annually, which is how much profit was made after calculating the income and expenses. This is also known as the profit and loss statement, and the primary purpose of this is to show if a company is profitable.

This statement is usually divided into a few sections, such as operating income, non-operating income, and operating expenses. The operating income deals primarily with the revenue associated with the core business model. For example, if company A makes smartphones, the first line in the income statement would be the revenue the business made from selling smartphones. After that, you would have the cost of goods sold, and this would be the material cost associated with actually building each of the phones the company sold. When you subtract the cost of goods sold from the total revenue, you get the value known as the gross margin, but there will be further expenses to deduct after this.

The cost of goods sold only considers the expenses from the materials needed to build smartphones, but the other costs, known as operating expenses, are not part of this. One of the most common examples you will see is known as SG&A, or selling, general, and administrative expenses. Things like advertising costs or the cost of the factory space needed to produce phones are included in SG&A. The next section of the income statement is dedicated to non-operating income. This is where you would see income not associated with the core business model. If this same smartphone company has unused space in their factory that they rent out to another company, the income from that transaction will appear in this section. This is because it is not directly associated with the primary business model of selling phones.

Something like the proceeds from a lawsuit or other infrequent income will be displayed under non-operating income as well. The benefit of these separate sections is that you can get a clear understanding of how a company's core business model is performing without being distracted by random sources of income. The income statement will show you the company's net income before and after taxes. You will also find its EPS (earnings per share), which, as was discussed earlier, is used to calculate multiples like the P/E ratio. The income statement is an excellent way to assess a business's profitability, see how it has grown over time, and predict how much it may still grow in the future.

Next is the cash flow statement, and this illustrates the flow of cash in and out of the organization. When looking for a possible investment, you want to ensure that the company has enough cash coming in so that the business can continue to operate. The cash flow statement is often split into three sections. First is the section labeled as cash flow from operations (CFO). This consists of the cash coming in and out of the company related to day to day, short term activities. For example, the cash received from regular customers and wages paid to employees on a bi-weekly basis. This illustrates how much money the company has made from its primary operations or its operating profit. Ideally, this number will be increasing year over year, which indicates that the business is growing. If the CFO is negative, the company is losing money, and this is not sustainable.

The second section is the cash flow from investing (CFI). This is where you would find capital expenditures (often abbreviated as CAPEX), and this is the cost the business accrues from buying new assets or maintaining its current ones. An example would be the maintenance of the company's fleet of vehicles, which it uses to conduct business operations or buying more land to build factories. Since the CFI is money spent maintaining or growing the business, the number in this section is typically negative. With that said, it may be positive if the business generates income from investments or selling assets. In this section, you may also see cash involved with acquisitions if the company buys part or all of another business.

The third section is the cash flow from financing (CFF). Here you will find items like debt, equity, and dividends. If the company took out a loan, which is debt, the monthly payments would fall under this section and the same for any dividends the business paid out to its investors. If the CFF is positive, this is usually an indicator that the business is raising money with a loan. In contrast, a negative CFF is when the company is paying money to its investors in the form of dividends or making payments to the loan.

One last thing to consider is something called free cash flow. This is not something you will find on the cash flow statement but is extremely important. It is calculated by taking the CFO and subtracting the capital expenditures found in the CFI. Free cash flow is the amount of money left over when the business pays all of its obligations and can be used for anything the company wants. You want to see this number growing over time as it shows the company can fund any activities to expand without the need to take on more debt.

The cash flow statement is often the preferred statement to look at when measuring performance because the ability to generate cash is imperative to the business's continued growth. When comparing the cash flow statement to the income statement, if the CFO is greater than the net income, this generally means that the company has a good quality of earnings. However, if they are equal, this means that the business is spending every dollar it makes just to stay in business, and therefore is unable to expand without taking out debt. Also, looking at the cash flow statement can show you if a company is operating successfully and can have a positive cash flow from operations while expanding and paying its obligations.

Next is the balance sheet, and the purpose of this is to show that the business is worth more than what it owes on its outstanding debts. This organizes a business's total assets, liabilities, and shareholder equity. The balance sheet differs from the previous two financial statements because it focuses on a fixed period in time rather than on a quarter or an entire year. Assets are split into current assets and noncurrent assets. Current assets are assets that are on a company's balance sheet, typically for a year or less. They include things like cash, inventories, and accounts receivable (money that will be received from customers soon). These are typically listed in order based on their degree of liquidity or how easily they are converted to cash, and therefore cash will be first.

After this, you will have the rest of the assets that either make the business money or are worth money, such as the real estate where their factory is located. Noncurrent assets are long-term assets that will be on the balance sheet for a long time. Using the smartphone company from the previous example, if that business purchases a new piece of equipment that allows it to manufacture smartphones faster and at a cheaper cost, that piece of equipment is a long-term asset and, therefore, a noncurrent asset. Noncurrent assets are often categorized as PP&E, or property, plants, and equipment.

Liabilities are debts the company must pay and are organized in the same manner, current and noncurrent, based on the short or long term. Current liabilities include accounts payable and accrued expenses. Accounts payable is money paid to suppliers for goods or services, and accrued expenses pay the company's employees. The most common example of a noncurrent liability is a long-term bank loan. For example, if a company borrows a billion dollars to build a new factory to manufacture products.

Finally, equity is the amount left over after you subtract the liabilities from the assets. You want to look for a positive number here, and this is what is referred to as positive working capital. In the equity section, you will find things like share capital, which is income earned from selling shares to investors. You may also see retained earnings, which is the amount of money a company keeps after expenses, including paying dividends to the investors. In this section, you will also see treasury stock, which is how much the business spent on buying back its shares.

This statement is called the balance sheet because everything must balance when you stack them side by side, with assets on one side and liabilities/shareholder equity on the other. The equation used for this is assets = liabilities + equity. When looking at a business's balance sheet, a good sign of a healthy company is when its equity is increasing. This shows that it is making enough profit to cover expenses, grow the business, and still increase its value. Another point to consider is that the ratio of assets versus liabilities is at least two to one, meaning that its total assets are worth at least twice the value of its total liabilities.

Finally, there is the annual report which can be found on the company's website. As the name implies, this form covers all of the annual financials of the company. This will typically start with a letter from the CEO or chairman and will address things like the business's successes over the year and areas that can be improved. The annual report will also include the remuneration report & incentives. Here you will find the incentives and/or compensation plans for the people who run the company, in the form of both long and short-term incentives.

The next few sections of the annual report are the financial statements that were covered earlier, the income statement, cash flow statement, and the balance sheet, and now you should have a basic understanding of how to read these. After these, you will see the notes and segment report. In the notes, you will find clarification on how the business generates the values you find in the financial statements, so if something does not look right to you, you may find clarification here. Under the notes section, you will find the segment report. If you are looking at a massive company that has many different businesses underneath the larger company, here, you will find the breakdown of all the different businesses and be able to see the performance of each one. The last section of the annual report will be the auditor's report/declaration. If a statement is audited, this typically means that something is not in compliance with accounting standards and can be a red flag if you are looking at this company as a potential investment.

The best place to get information on a company is from the company itself. The financial statements discussed can be found on the investor relations page of a business's website. Businesses will have short and long-term goals to expand the company and increase profitability. Each quarter, companies that trade publicly on the stock market will have an earning's call. This is where the leadership of the business will go over the performance for the previous quarter, how they did when compared to expectations, and how the company plans to continue growing over the coming years.

Earnings calls are often streamed online on multiple platforms, and in some cases, you can listen directly from your brokerage account. When planning to invest in a business, it is important to keep up with its performance, keep up with its quarterly earnings calls, and analyze its financial statements. In addition to tracking the business's performance, it can be helpful to keep up with the management team and how it operates. A great CEO and management team can cause a business to have explosive growth, while poor management can destroy a business. You want to see a leadership team that has talent and integrity.

Valuing stocks can be different based on the type of stock you are looking at. Arguably one of the most important types of stocks to understand is a growth stock. These are companies that grow exponentially, and while they tend to carry more risk in the early days, if you can see the long-term impact, these companies can have extremely high returns. Analysts misunderstand many growth companies because a lot of the metrics do not make sense when you try to value them by traditional metrics. Earlier in this book, it was discussed that many people think that a lower P/E ratio is best, so when you see a relatively young company with a P/E ratio of over one hundred, it simply looks ridiculously overvalued. Many people will not look any further. The key take-away is that you have to dig deeper when looking at these companies and understand that you cannot value a growth stock the same way as you would a value stock.

When looking at growth companies, you have to make educated and informed guesses about where you think the business will be in the coming years and decades. Looking at factors such as the potential market, size of the industry, and any competitive advantage it may have over the competition can help you reach conclusions about the business's future success. Growth stocks tend to be younger companies with a higher valuation, and there is usually a lot of volatility or fluctuation involved with the share price.

There can be many indicators for future success, but one significant phenomenon is called disruptive innovation. This is the result of a company redefining an entire market and subsequently taking the throne away from the larger businesses within the sector. Often, the new way of doing things is so fundamentally different from how the rest of the industry does things that the industry leaders are unable to compete because they would have to change their entire business model to do so. In many cases, they do not have enough time or money to restructure everything while still trying to make a profit. By the time the large businesses realize what is happening, they may have already been surpassed by that small startup company they failed to notice. This type of radical innovation often creates entirely new markets or permanently alters existing ones.

One of the most well-known examples of disruption within an industry is the evolution of Netflix. This company has evolved several times since its inception in 1997, and eventually, its IPO in 2002. At first, Netflix was a service where you could rent DVDs that you would receive and return via the mail. At this point, Netflix was going up against industry leaders like Blockbuster that had a business model that revolved around customers needing to go to a physical location to rent movies and paying late fees if they were unable to return the movies on time. (Caplinger, 2018).

Therefore, a service where you can send movies back in the mail was a lot more convenient for many customers, and video delivery as a whole was an innovation in this industry. Netflix also offered unlimited rentals with no late fees; this also helped the company take the lead over its competition. In 2007, it introduced video streaming and later on started to produce movies and shows specific to its platform. By this time, Netflix had forever changed the television industry, effectively putting many of its competitors out of business. This disruptive innovation made a lot of money for the investors who had a long-term vision of where the company could reach in the future. The chart below shows how the stock rose over the years. Every $1,000 invested at the IPO of Netflix in 2002 was worth $81,000 by 2016, as it rose about 8,000% within these fourteen years (Caplinger, 2018).

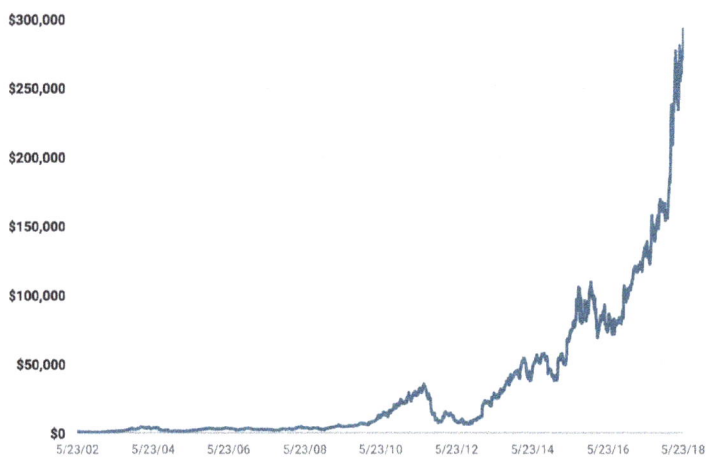

Value of $1,000 invested after Netflix's IPO

Source: Business Insider calculations using split-adjusted closing stock prices from Yahoo Finance

BUSINESS INSIDER

(Kiersz, 2018)

CULTIVATING AN INVESTOR MINDSET

According to an article from *Business Insider*, if a person had invested just $1,000 into Apple during its initial IPO back in 1980, assuming you invested nothing else, that position would be valued at over $8.9 million by 2018 (Kiersz, 2018). While it is true that not every company will turn into the next Apple, this example illustrates two fundamental principles. The first is something that was covered earlier; in most cases, the stock market is not a tool that can be used to get rich quickly. This scenario took almost forty years to get that kind of return. When talking about long term investing, these are the kinds of situations to have in mind.

The modern world is one built on instant gratification with things like online shopping and overnight shipping. Many people are not conditioned to wait for things they want, including making a lot of money. Some people reading that scenario may think that it is "not worth it" to wait for that kind of return, but the counter-argument for that thought process is this: Time will continue to pass regardless of what you do or do not do. Would you rather have almost $10 million when you are ready to retire or have to rely on social security checks to make ends meet?

The second principle illustrated in the previous example can be summed up with a prevalent mantra in investing circles, that time in the market beats timing the market. At some point, you have probably heard the advice to buy low and sell high. While this sounds great in theory, it does not consider that nobody can accurately predict what will happen in the stock market consistently. Trying to wait for a stock to go to its lowest is simply introducing more risk because while you are waiting, you could continue to miss out on the opportunity to buy into that company if the price of the stock steadily increases over time. Besides, if you sell at a "high" price, you can make some short-term profits, but if the company's stock more than triples within the following few years, you also miss out on more potential gains. Selling your investment for a profit should be based on the investment goals you set for yourself. Perhaps you want to reach a certain amount so that you can put a down payment on your dream home. In a scenario like this, even if the stock goes up more after you sell it, you were still able to reach your goal and get the money you needed from your investment.

Instead of trying to time the markets, using something called DCA (dollar-cost averaging) can be more beneficial in the long term. Dollar-cost averaging is simply when you consistently invest in the market without trying only to buy when the market dips. As seen in an article from *Market Watch*, wealth management analyst Nick Maggiulli analyzed several forty-year periods with two different investing approaches when investing in the S&P 500. In one scenario, you know in advance exactly the lowest points of each dip in the market, and in the other, you simply dollar cost average by investing consistently every month. He found that even with perfect knowledge on when the markets would be at their lowest, the DCA approach outperformed timing the markets over 70% of the time. In a realistic situation, you will not be able to accurately predict the very bottom of the market on every pullback, so your chances of beating DCA are even lower. So, if you wait on the sidelines to invest, you will likely miss out on major gains. The following graph illustrates the difference (Langlois, 2019).

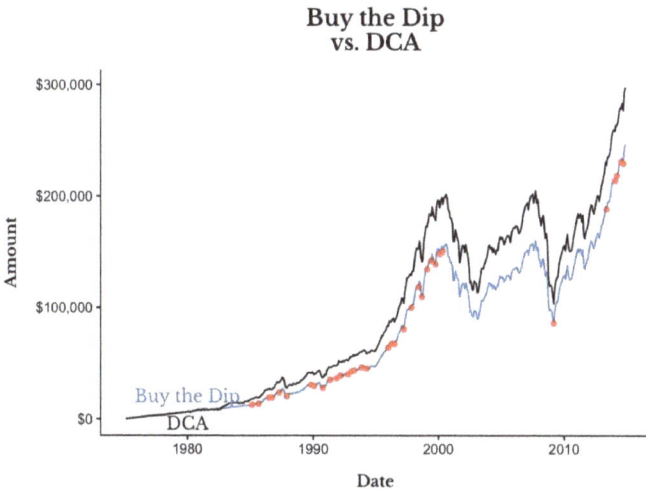

Buy the Dip vs. DCA

Source: http://www.econ.yale.edu/~shiller/data.htm (OfDollarsAndData.com)
Note: The Buy the Dip strategy accumulates cash and buys at 'dips' in the S&P 500. Real return includes reinvested dividends.

(Langlois, 2019)

According to an article from *The Motley Fool*, when looking at the period between January 1, 1999, to December 31, 2018, missing out on just ten of the best days during these twenty years would have cut your returns in half. This is how trying to time the market can potentially cost you a lot of money. Allowing the money to sit and grow can exponentially increase the amount of compound growth you can see within your portfolio (Aloi, 2019).

When it comes to long-term investing, keeping a level head is a key factor in minimizing risk. As mentioned previously, the stock market is based heavily on emotions, and this is what leads to a lot of the volatility seen in the market. Ups and downs are not only normal, but they are a sign of a healthy market. When you understand this, market dips should not scare you. When you sell at a loss during a bear market, you are locking in those losses and not giving your investments a chance to bounce back. If you are still a long way away from retirement, there is still plenty of time for things to transition back to a bull market and grow your portfolio.

To build wealth in the stock market, you must be able to recognize and seize excellent opportunities. By now, you have seen that this book mentions several times that the market goes up and down and that this is normal. While people can understand this concept, it is still natural to panic a bit during a bear market when you see your portfolio drop in value in a relatively short time. True investors keep their emotions in check and realize that this is an excellent opportunity to buy solid stocks at a discount, so to speak. During a bear market, many people will panic and sell all their investments to prevent further losses.

The stock market works on supply and demand, so when many people are selling, share prices decrease. When this happens, look at some of these companies fundamentally. Is there anything in their business model that changed to warrant a much lower stock price? Does this company have enough resources to survive a downturn, enough money on its balance sheet to get through a time where it may not generate revenue?

If the respective answers to these questions are "no" and "yes" and you believe this company will come back stronger after the bear market, this could be a great time to buy a secure business below its intrinsic value. In the following months or years, you could see a great return since you were able to not just refrain from panicking during the bear market but because you had the knowledge and conviction to buy more. This is summed up by an excellent quote from Warren Buffett, "Be greedy when others are fearful and fearful when others are greedy."

The second part of the quote from Mr. Buffett applies to the opposite situation. You may have heard of FOMO, the fear of missing out, and this can be very detrimental in the stock market. Every so often, a new popular stock will emerge, and it seems as if everyone is talking about this company. You may hear your friends and coworkers talking about this stock, and you see the stock price increase almost daily without fail. People will see others making money on this stock, and they do not want to miss out, so they buy into this stock.

This can cause a company to become overvalued or reach a price higher than its intrinsic value. In this scenario, the problem with FOMO is that people are assuming that the price of this stock only goes up, and this is simply untrue. Even the best stocks do not go up in a straight line, and a pullback every so often is a normal and pretty healthy thing. At the sign of a slight drop in the stock, those same people begin to panic and sell off all their shares. A chain reaction happens, and more people sell, causing the stock price to drop even further. This goes back to the point that the stock market is largely built on emotional reactions. Many of the people who buy stocks due to FOMO are typically not buying these companies based on that business's fundamentals or because they think the company will grow over the coming years; this is a good segway into the next factor in cultivating an investor mindset.

One of the most important principles in the world of investing is simply investing in companies that you fundamentally understand. There are two parts to this. First, it is important to understand why you are investing in a company, your financial goals, and how long you plan to hold that stock. Looking at the fundamentals discussed earlier and coming to your conclusion as to why you believe this company is a sound investment may sound simple, but many people do not approach investing in this manner.

You should have the conviction to buy and hold the companies you see as good investments, even when the stock may fluctuate in the short term. You can minimize your risk when you understand the business very well. Ideally, you should be able to justify why you believe in the company, understand the data that you are using to support your thesis, and understand why the business will continue to execute its plans over the coming months and years. Putting your money into a company's stock without fundamentally understanding the underlying business and its financials is not investing; it is gambling.

The second part of investing in businesses you understand comes down to understanding its products and how its products get to customers. Imagine a pharmaceutical company that is working on an extremely complex medical drug that can stop the effects of aging. Needless to say, the actual process of creating such a product is likely very intricate. Unless you have a degree in the medical field, it may be difficult to understand the actual competitive advantage that this particular company has over the other pharmaceutical companies working on the same drug. This company may prove to be a good investment if it can succeed before its competitors. However, unless you understand that type of medical research, it can be hard to determine which of these companies will succeed. If you understand a company and exactly what it does and how it accomplishes its goals, it will be easier to make an educated choice on what to invest in.

A concept you will continuously hear about in the world of investing is diversification. As defined earlier, this can reduce your risk because if one of the stocks in your portfolio dips, it will be offset by the other holdings you have in different sectors. This is why it can be a useful tool, especially for those just getting started with investing. However, diversification for its own sake may not be the best course of action. Would you rather be an investor with ten average companies or an investor in one outstanding business?

Investor Warren Buffet has taken the stance that diversification is less than ideal: "Diversification is a protection against ignorance," according to Buffett. "[It] makes very little sense for those who know what they're doing." If you build up a portfolio with over thirty stocks, it becomes increasingly more difficult and time-consuming to analyze and keep track of all of them for those who chose to be active investors. Reading financial statements and keeping up with the latest news for every single company would require more time and energy than the average person is willing to commit.

Using that time to find a few solid businesses to invest in can provide a much better return. If you can find the company that will become the next Netflix or Apple, this is way more beneficial than holding many other stocks (Kaufman, 2018).

The last point is that no matter who it is, no one can predict the market or guarantee a return. The markets are volatile, irrational, and emotional, and there is an incalculable number of variables that can affect the stock market. The best that investors can do is to make educated guesses on what is likely to happen based on the data and trends that can be analyzed. A company might report lower earnings than expected, and its stock may still increase. Another company may have a break-through, but if people do not understand why that is important, the stock might fall.

The point is that even the best market analysts will never know with 100% accuracy what will happen. It is also imperative to understand that no one can guarantee a certain return consistently, and if people tell you that they can, be extremely wary because it is likely some kind of scam. Even in the best examples, such as when looking at the returns of a stock like Netflix in the previous chapter, no stock will go up in a straight line. There will be both ups and downs, and in that Netflix scenario, the investors who sold their shares during the first downturn of the share price likely regretted doing so later.

CONCLUSION

In conclusion, the world of investing has many moving parts, and this book seeks to provide a good baseline point of reference. It is important that you understand your goals with investing and the best approach for you, as there is no one method of investing definitively the best. This book covered some of the benefits of investing, some key terms, how to get started with investing, the different types of investments, investing strategies, valuing stocks, and thinking like an intelligent investor. The stock market, and investing as a whole, can be an excellent method of building generational wealth. However, as with anything else, you must have a good knowledge of the fundamentals. The sooner you start investing, the more time you have to grow your wealth.

REFERENCES

Aloi, M. (2019, April 11). What Happens When You Miss the Best Days in the Stock Market? Retrieved October 09, 2020, from https://www.fool.com/ investing/2019/04/11/what-happens-when-you-miss-the-best-days-in-the-st.aspx

Amadeo, K. (2020, September 17). How Bad Is Inflation? Past, Present, Future. Retrieved October 09, 2020, from https://www.thebalance.com/u-s-inflation-rate-history-by-year-and-forecast-3306093

Bendell, N. (2020, January 05). Why Albert Einstein loved compound interest. Retrieved October 09, 2020, from https://www.ratecity.com.au/investment-funds/articles/albert-einstein-loved-compound-interest

Caplinger, D. (2016, July 11). Netflix Stock History: What You Need to Know. Retrieved October 09, 2020, from https://www.fool.com/investing/2016/07/11/ netflix-stock-history-what-you-need-to-know.aspx

Jackson, N. M. (2019, October 21). How Do the Short-Term and Long-Term Capital Gains Tax Rates

Compare? Retrieved October 09, 2020, from https://www.acorns.com/money-basics/taxes/short-term-capital-gains-tax-rate/

Kaufman, K. (2018, July 25). Here's Why Warren Buffett And Other Great Investors Don't Diversify. Retrieved October 09, 2020, from https://www.forbes.com/sites/karlkaufman/2018/07/24/heres-why-warren-buffett-and-other-great-investors-dont-diversify/

Kiersz, A. (2018, May 24). Netflix's IPO was 16 years ago Wednesday - here's how much you'd have made if you invested $1,000 back in the day. Retrieved December 01, 2020, from https://www.businessinsider.com/netflix-stock-price-ipo-16th-anniversary-2018-5

Kiersz, A. (2018, August 02). Apple just became the first $1 trillion US company – here's how much you'd have made if you invested $1,000 back in the day. Retrieved October 09, 2020, from https://www.businessinsider.com/apple-stock-price-1-trillion-market-cap-2018-8

Langlois, S. (2019, February 06). 'This is the last article you'll ever need to read on market timing,' analyst claims. Retrieved October 09, 2020, from https://www.marketwatch.com/story/this-is-the-last-article-youll-ever-need-to-read-on-market-timing-analyst-claims-2019-02-06

Pisani, B. (2019, March 15). Active fund managers trail the S&P 500 for the ninth year in a row in triumph for indexing. Retrieved October 9, 2020, from https://www.cnbc.com/2019/03/15/active-fund-managers-trail-the-sp-500-for-the-ninth-year-in-a-row-in-triumph-for-indexing.html

Saibil, J. (2020, August 15). If You Invested $10,000 in Netflix's IPO, This Is How Much Money You'd Have Now. Retrieved October 09, 2020, from https://www.fool.com/investing/2020/08/15/if-you-invested-10000-in-netflixs-ipo-this-is-how/

Santoli, M. (2017, June 19). The S&P 500 has already met its average return for a full year, but don't expect it to stay here. Retrieved October 09, 2020, from https://www-cnbc-com.cdn.ampproject.org/v/s/www.cnbc.com/amp/2017/06/18/the-sp-500-has-already-met-its-average-return-for-a-full-year.html?amp_js_v=a3

Speights, K. (2020, October 23). How to Calculate the Intrinsic Value of a Stock. Retrieved October 26, 2020, from https://www.fool.com/investing/how-to-invest/stocks/intrinsic-value/